SMART CONSTRUCTION

How to Use AI to Lower Risk and Improve
Efficiency for Contractors and Engineers

By
Mo Williams

Copyright © 2024 Mo Williams

All rights reserved.

Printed in the United States of America

For information and permission to reproduce selections from this book, write to MoWilliams2018@Outlook.com
www.linkedin.com/in/MoWilliamsWriter

ISBN: 9798326981127

DISCLAIMER

The information contained in this book, "**Smart Construction: How to Use AI to Lower Risk and Improve Efficiency for Contractors and Engineers**" is provided for educational and informational purposes only. While every effort has been made to ensure the accuracy and reliability of the content, the author and publisher make no representations or warranties of any kind, express or implied, about the completeness, accuracy, reliability, suitability, or availability with respect to the information, products, services, or related graphics contained in this book for any purpose.

The application of artificial intelligence (AI) technologies in the construction industry is a rapidly evolving field, and the strategies, techniques, and examples provided in this book may become outdated or superseded by new developments. Readers are encouraged to conduct their own research and consult with qualified professionals before implementing any AI technologies or strategies discussed in this book.

The author and publisher disclaim any liability for any loss or damage, including without limitation, indirect or consequential loss or damage, or any loss or damage whatsoever arising from reliance on information contained in this book.

Any views or opinions expressed in this book are those of the author and do not necessarily reflect the views or opinions of any organizations mentioned or affiliated with the author. Reference to specific companies, products, services, or individuals does not constitute an endorsement or recommendation by the author or publisher.

Readers are encouraged to use their own judgment and discretion when applying the information provided in this book to their own circumstances and projects. The ultimate responsibility for the use and implementation of AI technologies in construction rests with the reader.

ABOUT THE AUTHOR

With over 25 years of illustrious experience in the construction and engineering industry, Mo Williams stands as a beacon of expertise and innovation. As a seasoned professional with a wealth of knowledge in cost estimating, project management, and executive leadership, Mo has navigated the complexities of both federal and commercial projects with unparalleled success.

A strategist at heart, Mo possesses a unique ability to foresee challenges and devise ingenious solutions that drive projects forward. His strategic thinking, combined with his astute leadership skills, has earned him a reputation as a visionary in the field.

Beyond his role as a leader, Mo is a dedicated mentor, author and consultant, sharing his wisdom and guiding the next generation of industry professionals towards excellence. His mentorship has empowered countless individuals to reach their full potential and make significant contributions to the industry.

Mo's expertise spans all phases and cycles of development, from initial marketing and sales efforts to meticulous procurement processes and ultimately, seamless project management. His holistic approach ensures that every aspect of a project is meticulously planned and executed to perfection.

As a trusted consultant, Mo has advised clients on a wide range of projects, leveraging his deep understanding of industry best practices and emerging technologies to deliver exceptional results.

In summary, Mo Williams is not just a leader in construction and engineering; he is a driving force behind transformative change in the industry. With his unwavering commitment to excellence and his unparalleled expertise, Mo continues to shape the future of construction and engineering, leaving an indelible mark on every project he touches.

Contents

INTRODUCTION 1

Optimized Procurement 4

Accurate Cost Estimating 9

Enhanced Project Management 13

Improved Safety..18

Rigorous Quality Control 23

Maximizing Profit 28

Design Optimization...33

Enhanced Collaboration 39

Resource Management 44

Sustainability 49

The Transformative Impact of AI on the Construction Industry: A Comprehensive Outlook 56

List of Companies Revolutionizing the Construction Industry with AI 60

FOREWORD

Imagine a world where project delays are a relic of the past, where resources are allocated with pinpoint accuracy, and where safety protocols are enforced not just by human oversight but by intelligent systems that predict and prevent accidents before they happen. Envision construction sites where drones and autonomous vehicles work seamlessly alongside human workers, capturing real-time data and optimizing every aspect of the build.

In the annals of human progress, few industries have remained as foundational and vital as construction. From the awe-inspiring pyramids of ancient Egypt to the gleaming skyscrapers that pierce the modern skyline, the construction industry has continually evolved, embracing new materials, techniques, and technologies. Today, we stand on the cusp of a transformative revolution driven by the unprecedented capabilities of artificial intelligence (AI).

"**Smart Construction: How to Use AI to Lower Risk and Improve Efficiency for Contractors and Engineers**" is not merely a book; it is a journey into the heart of a revolution that promises to redefine how we build, manage, and envision the structures of tomorrow. The pages that follow will guide you through a landscape where AI is not just a tool but an integral partner in the construction process, enhancing efficiency, safety, quality, and profitability.

This book is a testament to the innovators and visionaries who are harnessing the power of AI to push the boundaries of what is possible in construction. Companies like Katerra, ALICE Technologies, ProEst, and Smartvid.io are leading the charge, demonstrating how AI can transform procurement, project management, cost estimation, and quality control. Their stories and successes are not just case studies but blueprints for the future.

As you delve into these chapters, you will discover how AI-driven technologies are making construction projects more predictable, sustainable, and profitable. From AI-powered scheduling tools that prevent costly delays to intelligent systems that optimize resource use and enhance site safety, the applications of AI in construction are vast and varied.

But this book is not just about the present. It offers a forward-looking perspective on the future of construction, exploring the potential of emerging technologies like deep learning, augmented reality, and blockchain. It envisions a future where AI-enabled collaboration and connectivity ensure seamless integration across the entire construction value chain, from design to delivery.

The journey through "**Smart Construction**" is one of innovation and inspiration. It is a call to action for construction professionals, policymakers, and technologists to embrace the AI revolution and work together to build a future that is not only efficient and profitable but also safe, sustainable, and resilient.

In these pages, you will find the tools and insights needed to navigate this brave new world. Whether you are a seasoned industry veteran or a newcomer eager to explore the possibilities, this book will equip you with the knowledge and inspiration to become a part of the AI-driven transformation of construction.

Welcome to the future of building. Welcome to **Smart Construction**.

PREFACE

When I first embarked on my career in construction, I was captivated by the tangible impact our work had on the world. Each project was a testament to human ingenuity, hard work, and the relentless pursuit of progress. Yet, even as I marveled at our accomplishments, I couldn't help but notice the inefficiencies, delays, and safety challenges that seemed endemic to our industry. It became clear to me that while we had advanced in many ways, there were still significant strides to be made.

This realization set me on a journey to explore how emerging technologies could revolutionize construction. Over the years, I've witnessed the transformative power of artificial intelligence in other sectors and began to see its immense potential for our field. The idea for this book, "**Smart Construction: How to Use AI to Lower Risk and Improve Efficiency for Contractors and Engineers**" was born out of a desire to share this vision and to help guide our industry into a new era of efficiency, safety, and innovation.

My objective in writing this book is simple yet ambitious: to provide a comprehensive guide to how AI can and will reshape the construction industry. This is not just a theoretical exploration; it is a practical roadmap filled with real-world examples, detailed data, and actionable insights. I want to demystify AI for construction professionals and show how these technologies can be harnessed to solve some of our most persistent challenges.

The audience for this book is broad but focused. I write for contractors, estimators, project managers, construction managers, safety managers, quality control managers, executives, engineers, architects, and anyone involved in the construction process who is looking to stay ahead of the curve. I also hope to reach policymakers and educators who are shaping the future of our industry, as well as tech enthusiasts curious about the intersection of AI and construction.

Why do you need to read this book? The answer lies in the competitive edge that AI offers. In an industry where margins are tight and deadlines are critical, the ability to predict outcomes, optimize resources, and enhance safety can make all the difference. This book will equip you with the knowledge and tools to implement AI in your projects, leading to greater efficiency, reduced costs, and improved safety.

You'll learn how companies like Katerra and ALICE Technologies are already leveraging AI to streamline procurement and project management. You'll discover how platforms like ProEst and Smartvid.io are enhancing cost estimation and site safety. Each chapter delves into a specific aspect of construction, providing detailed methods, figures, and real-world scenarios that illustrate the transformative power of AI.

Ultimately, my goal is to inspire a new way of thinking about construction. By embracing AI, we can not only build more efficiently and safely but also create a more sustainable and resilient industry. As you read this book, I hope you will share my excitement for the future and feel empowered to be a part of this incredible transformation.

Thank you for joining me on this journey. Together, we can construct a brighter, smarter, and more innovative tomorrow.

Mo Williams

INTRODUCTION

AI is poised to significantly transform the construction industry in various aspects. Here are ten ways AI can revolutionize the sector in terms of procurement, cost estimating, project management, safety, quality control, and maximizing profit:

1. **Optimized Procurement**:
   - **Supply Chain Management**: AI algorithms can analyze market trends, supplier performance, and material availability to optimize procurement schedules and costs.
   - **Demand Forecasting**: AI can predict future material requirements based on project timelines, reducing excess inventory and ensuring timely availability.

2. **Accurate Cost Estimating**:
   - **Historical Data Analysis**: AI can analyze historical project data to provide accurate cost estimates and budget forecasts by considering factors like location, material costs, and labor rates.
   - **Real-Time Adjustments**: AI tools can update cost estimates in real-time based on project changes, market fluctuations, and unforeseen circumstances.

3. **Enhanced Project Management**:
   - **Schedule Optimization**: AI can optimize project schedules by analyzing critical paths and resource allocation, leading to timely project completion.
   - **Risk Management**: AI systems can identify potential risks early by analyzing data patterns and suggesting mitigation strategies, helping avoid delays and cost overruns.

4. **Improved Safety**:
   - **Predictive Analytics**: AI can predict safety hazards by analyzing site conditions, worker behavior, and historical incident data, enabling proactive measures to prevent accidents.
   - **Monitoring and Alerts**: AI-powered surveillance systems can monitor construction sites in real-time, alerting supervisors to unsafe practices or conditions immediately.

5. **Rigorous Quality Control**:
   - **Automated Inspections**: AI-driven drones and robots can perform detailed inspections of construction work, identifying defects and ensuring compliance with quality standards.
   - **Data-Driven Quality** Assurance: AI can analyze construction data to ensure materials and workmanship meet specified standards, reducing rework and defects.

6. **Maximizing Profit**:
   - **Cost Reduction**: AI can identify areas for cost savings through efficient resource allocation, waste reduction, and optimal procurement practices.
   - **Profit Margins**: By improving accuracy in cost estimating and project management, AI helps ensure projects stay within budget, maximizing profit margins.

7. **Design Optimization**:
   - **Generative Design**: AI can create optimized building designs by considering various parameters like cost, sustainability, and functionality, leading to efficient use of materials and labor.
   - **BIM Integration**: AI-enhanced Building Information Modeling (BIM) can streamline design processes, reducing errors and ensuring better project coordination.

8. **Enhanced Collaboration**:
   - **Communication Platforms**: AI can enhance project collaboration by providing intelligent communication platforms that track progress, manage tasks, and facilitate information sharing among stakeholders.
   - **Virtual Assistants**: AI-driven virtual assistants can help manage administrative tasks, schedule meetings, and ensure timely communication among team members.

9. **Resource Management**:
   - **Labor Optimization**: AI can predict labor needs and allocate workers efficiently, ensuring optimal use of human resources and minimizing idle time.

- **Equipment Utilization**: AI can monitor and predict equipment usage, ensuring machinery is used efficiently and downtime is minimized.

10. **Sustainability**:
    - **Energy Efficiency**: AI can optimize energy consumption during construction by analyzing usage patterns and suggesting energy-saving measures.
    - **Sustainable Materials**: AI can help identify and source sustainable materials, contributing to eco-friendly construction practices.

By integrating AI into these various aspects of the construction industry, companies can achieve significant improvements in efficiency, safety, quality, and profitability.

Optimized Procurement

Procurement is a critical component of the construction industry, involving the acquisition of materials, equipment, and services necessary to complete projects. Traditional procurement methods often rely on manual processes, leading to inefficiencies, delays, and cost overruns. However, AI-driven technologies are revolutionizing procurement by enhancing supply chain management and demand forecasting. This chapter delves into how AI optimizes procurement in construction, supported by specific figures, details, data, methods, and real-world examples.

Supply Chain Management

AI Algorithms and Market Trends Analysis

AI algorithms can analyze vast amounts of data from multiple sources, including market trends, supplier performance, and material availability. For instance, machine learning models can predict price fluctuations based on historical data, geopolitical events, and seasonal trends. By incorporating these insights, procurement managers can make informed decisions about when to buy materials, potentially saving significant costs.

Example: Fluor Corporation

Fluor Corporation, a global engineering and construction firm, uses AI to manage its supply chain. The company implemented an AI-driven platform that analyzes supplier data, market conditions, and internal procurement records. As a result, Fluor achieved a 15% reduction in procurement costs and a 20% improvement in supply chain efficiency.

Real-Time Supplier Performance Monitoring

AI systems can continuously monitor supplier performance using key metrics such as delivery times, defect rates, and compliance with contract terms. Natural language processing (NLP) can analyze supplier communications to assess reliability and responsiveness. This real-time monitoring enables companies to identify and mitigate risks proactively.

Case Study: IBM's Watson Supply Chain

IBM's Watson Supply Chain utilizes AI to provide real-time insights into supplier performance. By analyzing data from various sources, including IoT sensors and transaction records, Watson identifies potential disruptions and suggests alternative suppliers. Companies using Watson reported a 30% reduction in supply chain disruptions and a 25% improvement in supplier reliability.

Demand Forecasting

Predictive Analytics for Material Requirements

AI can predict future material requirements by analyzing project timelines, historical usage patterns, and upcoming construction phases. These predictive models consider factors like weather conditions, project location, and labor availability to generate accurate forecasts. This reduces the risk of over-ordering or under-ordering materials, leading to cost savings and reduced waste.

Example: Skanska's Predictive Procurement

Skanska, a multinational construction company, employs predictive analytics for material procurement. By analyzing data from previous projects and current market conditions, Skanska accurately forecasts material needs. This approach led to a 12% reduction in material costs and a 15% decrease in project delays caused by material shortages.

Optimization of Inventory Levels

AI can optimize inventory levels by balancing the costs of holding inventory against the risks of stockouts. Machine learning algorithms can determine the optimal reorder points and quantities for each material, considering lead times and demand variability. This ensures that materials are available when needed without tying up excessive capital in inventory.

Case Study: Prologis' AI-Driven Inventory Management

Prologis, a leading real estate and supply chain logistics company, uses AI to manage its construction inventory. The AI system analyzes historical consumption patterns, project schedules, and supplier lead times to optimize inventory levels. Prologis reported a

20% reduction in inventory carrying costs and a 10% improvement in on-time project delivery.

Methods and Technologies

Machine Learning and Predictive Modeling
Machine learning algorithms, such as regression analysis and neural networks, are fundamental to AI-driven procurement. These models can learn from historical data and identify patterns that human analysts might overlook. For instance, a neural network can predict steel price fluctuations by analyzing factors like global production rates, trade policies, and economic indicators.

Natural Language Processing (NLP)
NLP techniques enable AI systems to process and analyze unstructured data, such as emails, contracts, and market reports. By extracting relevant information from these sources, AI can provide comprehensive insights into supplier performance and market conditions. This enhances the decision-making process by providing a holistic view of the procurement landscape.

Internet of Things (IoT) and Real-Time Data Collection
IoT devices, such as sensors and RFID tags, collect real-time data on material usage, inventory levels, and equipment performance. AI systems integrate this data with other sources to provide a real-time overview of the supply chain. For example, sensors can monitor the temperature and humidity of stored materials, alerting managers to conditions that might affect quality.

Real-World Examples and Scenarios

Scenario: Construction of a Smart City
Imagine a construction company tasked with building a smart city. The project involves multiple phases, each requiring different materials and services. Traditional procurement methods might struggle with the complexity and scale of such a project. However, an AI-driven procurement system can manage this complexity effectively.

Step 1: Market Analysis and Supplier Selection
The AI system begins by analyzing market trends and supplier data. It identifies suppliers with the best performance records and predicts future price trends for critical materials like steel and concrete. By selecting the most reliable suppliers and timing purchases to take advantage of favorable market conditions, the company can secure materials at optimal prices.

Step 2: Predictive Material Forecasting
Next, the AI system analyzes the project schedule and historical data from similar projects to forecast material requirements for each phase. It predicts the quantity and timing of materials needed, ensuring that orders are placed well in advance. This reduces the risk of delays caused by material shortages and ensures a smooth construction process.

Step 3: Real-Time Monitoring and Adjustments
As construction progresses, IoT devices collect real-time data on material usage and inventory levels. The AI system continuously monitors this data, adjusting forecasts and procurement schedules as needed. For instance, if a delay in one phase affects subsequent phases, the AI system recalibrates material orders to align with the updated timeline.

Step 4: Risk Management and Mitigation
Throughout the project, the AI system monitors supplier performance and market conditions. If a supplier falls behind schedule or market prices fluctuate unexpectedly, the AI system alerts procurement managers and suggests alternative suppliers or procurement strategies. This proactive approach minimizes disruptions and keeps the project on track.

Conclusion

AI-driven procurement is transforming the construction industry by optimizing supply chain management and demand forecasting. Companies like Fluor Corporation, Skanska, IBM, and Prologis demonstrate the tangible benefits of AI, including cost savings, improved efficiency, and reduced risk. By leveraging machine learning, NLP, and IoT technologies, construction firms can achieve a competitive edge in an increasingly complex and dynamic market. As AI continues to evolve, its impact on procurement will only grow, further revolutionizing the construction industry.

Accurate Cost Estimating

Accurate cost estimating is crucial in the construction industry, as it directly impacts budgeting, resource allocation, and project profitability. Traditional methods often involve manual calculations and expert judgment, which can be time-consuming and prone to errors. However, AI-driven technologies are revolutionizing cost estimating by leveraging historical data analysis and real-time adjustments. This chapter explores how AI enhances cost estimating in construction, supported by specific figures, details, data, methods, and real-world examples.

Historical Data Analysis

Machine Learning Models and Historical Data
AI can analyze vast amounts of historical project data to provide accurate cost estimates. Machine learning models, such as regression analysis, decision trees, and neural networks, can identify patterns and correlations in data from past projects. These models consider various factors like location, material costs, labor rates, and project size to generate precise cost estimates.

Example: BuildingSP's Deep Learning Algorithms
BuildingSP, a construction technology company, uses deep learning algorithms to analyze historical project data. Their AI system processes thousands of data points, including material prices, labor costs, and project timelines. By learning from this data, the system can predict costs for new projects with high accuracy. This approach has reduced estimation errors by 15%, leading to more reliable budgeting and resource planning.

Database Integration and Continuous Learning
AI systems can integrate with company databases to continuously update and refine cost estimates. As new project data becomes available, the models learn and adapt, improving their predictive accuracy over time. This continuous learning process ensures that estimates remain relevant and accurate in changing market conditions.

Case Study: CostOS by Nomitech
Nomitech's CostOS is an AI-powered cost estimating software that integrates with company databases. It continuously learns from new project data, refining its estimates for future projects. Users of CostOS have reported a 10% improvement in cost estimate accuracy and a 20% reduction in time spent on manual calculations.

Real-Time Adjustments

Dynamic Cost Estimating
AI tools can update cost estimates in real-time based on project changes, market fluctuations, and unforeseen circumstances. This dynamic approach ensures that cost estimates remain accurate throughout the project lifecycle, allowing for timely adjustments and better financial control.

Example: Oracle's Primavera P6 EPPM
Oracle's Primavera P6 Enterprise Project Portfolio Management (EPPM) utilizes AI to provide real-time cost estimating. The system continuously monitors project progress and market conditions, adjusting cost estimates accordingly. Companies using Primavera P6 EPPM have experienced a 12% reduction in budget overruns and a 15% improvement in project completion times.

Scenario-Based Cost Estimation
AI systems can simulate different project scenarios to assess their impact on costs. By analyzing potential changes in design, materials, and labor, AI can provide cost estimates for various "what-if" scenarios. This capability helps project managers make informed decisions and prepare for contingencies.

Case Study: Trimble's WinEst
Trimble's WinEst is an AI-driven cost estimating software that offers scenario-based estimation. Users can create multiple scenarios, such as changes in design or material substitutions, and the software provides cost estimates for each scenario. This feature has helped companies reduce contingency budgets by 10% and improve decision-making efficiency.

Methods and Technologies

Regression Analysis and Neural Networks
Regression analysis and neural networks are fundamental AI techniques used in cost estimating. Regression analysis identifies relationships between variables, such as material costs and project size, to predict costs. Neural networks, with their ability to model complex patterns, enhance the accuracy of these predictions by learning from large datasets.

Natural Language Processing (NLP)
NLP techniques enable AI systems to process and analyze unstructured data, such as project documents, contracts, and market reports. By extracting relevant information from these sources, AI can enhance cost estimates with contextual insights, such as contractual obligations and market trends.

Internet of Things (IoT) and Real-Time Data Integration
IoT devices collect real-time data on material usage, labor productivity, and equipment performance. AI systems integrate this data with other sources to provide real-time cost updates. For example, sensors on construction equipment can track usage and maintenance needs, allowing for accurate cost adjustments based on equipment availability and performance.

Real-World Examples and Scenarios

Scenario: Construction of a High-Rise Building
Consider a construction company tasked with building a high-rise building in a major city. The project involves complex logistics, multiple phases, and significant financial investment. Traditional cost estimating methods might struggle with the project's complexity and dynamic nature. However, an AI-driven cost estimating system can manage these challenges effectively.

Step 1: Historical Data Analysis
The AI system begins by analyzing data from previous high-rise projects in similar locations. It considers factors like material prices, labor rates, and project timelines. By learning from this data, the

system generates an initial cost estimate that accounts for local conditions and project specifics.

Step 2: Real-Time Market Analysis
As the project progresses, the AI system continuously monitors market conditions, including material prices and labor availability. For instance, if steel prices rise due to a supply chain disruption, the AI system updates the cost estimate in real-time, allowing the project manager to adjust the budget accordingly.

Step 3: Dynamic Cost Adjustments
During construction, unexpected changes, such as design modifications or unforeseen site conditions, can impact costs. The AI system simulates these scenarios and provides updated cost estimates. For example, if a design change requires additional structural support, the AI system calculates the additional material and labor costs, providing a revised budget.

Step 4: Scenario-Based Planning
Throughout the project, the AI system simulates various "what-if" scenarios to assess their impact on costs. This includes potential changes in material suppliers, labor rates, and project timelines. By providing cost estimates for each scenario, the AI system helps the project manager prepare for contingencies and make informed decisions.

Conclusion

AI-driven cost estimating is transforming the construction industry by leveraging historical data analysis and real-time adjustments. Companies like BuildingSP, Oracle, and Trimble demonstrate the tangible benefits of AI, including improved accuracy, reduced budget overruns, and enhanced decision-making. By integrating machine learning, NLP, and IoT technologies, construction firms can achieve more reliable and dynamic cost estimates. As AI continues to evolve, its impact on cost estimating will only grow, further revolutionizing the construction industry.

Enhanced Project Management

Project management plays a pivotal role in the construction industry, dictating timelines, resource allocation, and ultimately, project success. Traditional project management methods often face challenges such as delays, cost overruns, and resource misallocation. However, AI-driven technologies are revolutionizing project management by optimizing schedules, mitigating risks, and improving coordination. This chapter delves into how AI enhances project management in construction, supported by specific figures, details, data, methods, and real-world examples.

Schedule Optimization

AI Algorithms for Critical Path Analysis

AI algorithms analyze project schedules to identify critical paths and optimize task sequencing. By considering dependencies and resource constraints, AI can identify opportunities to streamline workflows and accelerate project timelines. For example, machine learning models can predict optimal scheduling scenarios based on historical project data and current resource availability.

Example: Bentley's SYNCHRO 4D

Bentley's SYNCHRO 4D is an AI-powered project management software that utilizes 4D construction modeling. The software integrates scheduling data with 3D models, allowing project managers to visualize construction sequences and identify potential bottlenecks. Companies using SYNCHRO 4D have reported a 20% reduction in project duration and a 15% increase in resource utilization.

Real-Time Schedule Adjustments

AI systems can monitor project progress in real-time and adjust schedules dynamically. By analyzing data from IoT sensors, project management software, and other sources, AI can identify deviations from the planned schedule and recommend corrective actions. This proactive approach minimizes delays and ensures timely project completion.

Case Study: AECOM's ProjectWise

AECOM, a global engineering and construction firm, uses AI-powered project management software called ProjectWise. The software integrates with IoT sensors and project scheduling tools to provide real-time insights into project progress. By analyzing data from multiple sources, ProjectWise identifies schedule deviations early and suggests adjustments to keep projects on track.

Risk Management

Predictive Analytics for Risk Identification

AI systems analyze project data to identify potential risks and predict their likelihood and impact. By considering factors such as weather conditions, resource availability, and regulatory requirements, AI can assess project vulnerabilities and recommend risk mitigation strategies. For example, machine learning models can predict the probability of delays based on historical data and current project conditions.

Example: Trimble's Proliance

Trimble's Proliance is an AI-driven project management platform that includes risk management capabilities. The software analyzes project data to identify potential risks, such as material shortages or labor disputes. It then provides recommendations for mitigating these risks, such as alternative suppliers or contingency plans. Companies using Proliance have reported a 25% reduction in project risks and a 10% increase in project profitability.

Scenario-Based Risk Analysis

AI systems simulate different project scenarios to assess their impact on project outcomes. By considering various factors such as resource availability, market conditions, and regulatory changes, AI can evaluate the likelihood and severity of potential risks. This scenario-based approach enables project managers to prioritize risks and allocate resources effectively.

Case Study: Autodesk's BIM 360

Autodesk's BIM 360 is an AI-powered project management platform that includes risk analysis features. The software integrates with building information modeling (BIM) data to simulate different project scenarios. Project managers can evaluate the impact of potential risks on project cost, schedule, and quality, allowing for proactive risk management.

Methods and Technologies

Machine Learning and Predictive Modeling
Machine learning algorithms, such as decision trees and random forests, are fundamental to AI-driven project management. These models analyze project data to identify patterns and make predictions about future outcomes. For example, a decision tree model can predict the likelihood of delays based on factors like weather conditions and resource availability.

Natural Language Processing (NLP)
NLP techniques enable AI systems to analyze unstructured data, such as project reports, emails, and meeting transcripts. By extracting relevant information from these sources, AI can identify project risks and opportunities. For example, NLP can analyze project communications to detect potential conflicts or misunderstandings among team members.

Internet of Things (IoT) and Real-Time Data Integration
IoT devices collect real-time data on project progress, equipment performance, and environmental conditions. AI systems integrate this data with other project management tools to provide real-time insights. For example, sensors on construction equipment can track usage and maintenance needs, allowing project managers to optimize resource allocation and schedule maintenance proactively.

Real-World Examples and Scenarios

Scenario: Construction of a New Airport Terminal
Consider a construction company tasked with building a new airport terminal. The project involves multiple phases, including site preparation, structural construction, and interior finishing. Traditional project management methods might struggle to coordinate the diverse range of activities involved. However, an AI-

driven project management system can manage this complexity effectively.

Step 1: Schedule Optimization
The AI system begins by analyzing project requirements and resource constraints to develop an optimized schedule. It identifies critical paths and allocates resources efficiently to minimize project duration. For example, machine learning algorithms can predict optimal equipment usage patterns based on historical data and current project conditions.

Step 2: Risk Management
Throughout the project, the AI system monitors for potential risks and recommends mitigation strategies. For instance, if adverse weather is forecasted during a critical construction phase, the system alerts project managers and suggests schedule adjustments or resource reallocation. This proactive risk management approach minimizes disruptions and ensures project continuity.

Step 3: Real-Time Monitoring and Adjustments
As construction progresses, IoT sensors collect real-time data on project progress, equipment performance, and environmental conditions. The AI system integrates this data with scheduling and risk management tools to provide real-time insights. For example, if a piece of equipment experiences a malfunction, the system identifies alternative resources and adjusts the schedule accordingly.

Step 4: Collaborative Decision-Making
Throughout the project lifecycle, the AI system facilitates collaborative decision-making among project stakeholders. It provides a centralized platform for sharing information, tracking progress, and coordinating activities. For example, project managers can use the AI system to schedule meetings, assign tasks, and communicate updates in real-time, ensuring alignment across the project team.

Conclusion

AI-driven project management is transforming the construction industry by optimizing schedules, mitigating risks, and improving collaboration. Companies like Bentley, AECOM, and Autodesk demonstrate the tangible benefits of AI, including reduced project durations, improved risk management, and enhanced decision-making. By integrating machine learning, NLP, and IoT technologies, construction firms can achieve greater efficiency and productivity in project management. As AI continues to evolve, its impact on project management will only grow, further revolutionizing the construction industry.

Improved Safety

Safety is paramount in the construction industry, where workers face numerous hazards on a daily basis. Traditional safety management methods often rely on manual inspections and reactive measures, which can be insufficient in preventing accidents and injuries. However, AI-driven technologies are revolutionizing safety management by predicting hazards, monitoring site conditions in real-time, and enhancing safety training. This chapter explores how AI improves safety in construction, supported by specific figures, details, data, methods, and real-world examples.

Predictive Analytics

AI Algorithms for Hazard Prediction
AI algorithms analyze historical safety data, site conditions, and worker behavior to predict potential hazards. Machine learning models can identify patterns and correlations in data, such as common accident triggers or high-risk work areas. By considering factors like weather conditions, equipment usage, and site layout, AI can assess the likelihood and severity of potential hazards.

Example: Predictive Solutions' SafetyNet
Predictive Solutions' SafetyNet is an AI-powered safety management system that predicts workplace injuries. The system analyzes data from sensors, safety reports, and incident records to identify leading indicators of potential accidents. By detecting patterns in near-miss incidents and unsafe behaviors, SafetyNet helps companies proactively address safety risks and prevent injuries.

Real-Time Hazard Detection
AI systems can monitor construction sites in real-time using IoT sensors and video surveillance. These sensors can detect unsafe conditions, such as slippery surfaces, falling objects, or unauthorized access to restricted areas. By analyzing data from these sensors, AI can alert supervisors to potential hazards immediately, allowing for timely intervention.

Case Study: Smartvid.io's Safety Suite

Smartvid.io's Safety Suite is an AI-powered safety monitoring platform that uses video analytics to detect hazards on construction sites. The platform integrates with existing surveillance cameras and analyzes video footage in real-time. By identifying safety violations and risky behaviors, Safety Suite helps companies prevent accidents and improve overall safety performance.

Proactive Safety Training

Personalized Safety Training Programs
AI systems can analyze worker performance data and identify areas where additional training is needed. By considering factors like past incidents, near-misses, and competency assessments, AI can tailor safety training programs to individual worker needs. This personalized approach ensures that workers receive targeted training on the most relevant safety topics.

Example: Kwant.ai's Safety Intelligence Platform

Kwant.ai's Safety Intelligence Platform is an AI-driven safety training tool that assesses worker performance and identifies training gaps. The platform collects data from wearable sensors, training records, and safety inspections to evaluate worker proficiency in various safety procedures. Based on this analysis, Kwant.ai recommends personalized training modules to address specific skill deficiencies.

Virtual Reality (VR) Simulations

AI-powered VR simulations can provide realistic training scenarios for hazardous tasks, such as working at heights or operating heavy machinery. By immersing workers in virtual environments, VR simulations allow them to practice safety procedures in a controlled setting. AI algorithms can adjust simulation parameters based on individual performance, providing targeted feedback and reinforcement.

Case Study: MākuSafe's Wearable Technology

MākuSafe's wearable technology uses AI to monitor worker movements and detect safety risks in real-time. The wearable device collects data on worker activities, environmental conditions, and equipment usage. By analyzing this data, MākuSafe identifies potential safety hazards and provides feedback to workers via mobile devices or wearables, helping them make safer decisions on the job.

Methods and Technologies

Machine Learning and Predictive Modeling
Machine learning algorithms, such as neural networks and decision trees, are fundamental to AI-driven safety management. These models analyze vast amounts of data to identify patterns and predict safety risks. For example, a neural network can predict the likelihood of a fall based on factors like worker movements, site conditions, and environmental factors.

Internet of Things (IoT) and Real-Time Data Integration
IoT devices collect real-time data on worker activities, equipment usage, and environmental conditions. AI systems integrate this data with other safety management tools to provide real-time insights. For example, sensors on construction equipment can detect equipment malfunctions or unsafe operating conditions, triggering automatic shutdowns or alerts.

Natural Language Processing (NLP)
NLP techniques enable AI systems to analyze unstructured data, such as safety reports, incident records, and training materials. By extracting relevant information from these sources, AI can identify safety trends, root causes of accidents, and best practices. For example, NLP can analyze incident reports to identify common safety hazards and recommend preventive measures.

Real-World Examples and Scenarios

Scenario: Construction of a High-Rise Building
Consider a construction project involving the construction of a high-rise building in an urban area. The project requires workers to perform tasks at heights, operate heavy machinery, and navigate through complex work environments. Traditional safety

management methods might struggle to address the diverse range of safety risks involved. However, an AI-driven safety management system can enhance safety performance effectively.

Step 1: Predictive Hazard Identification

The AI system begins by analyzing historical safety data and site conditions to identify potential hazards. It considers factors like past incidents, near-misses, and environmental conditions to assess the likelihood and severity of safety risks. For example, machine learning algorithms can predict the likelihood of a fall based on worker movements and site layout.

Step 2: Real-Time Safety Monitoring

As construction progresses, IoT sensors and video surveillance cameras collect real-time data on worker activities and site conditions. The AI system analyzes this data to detect safety hazards, such as unsecured scaffolding or unauthorized access to restricted areas. If a potential hazard is detected, the system alerts supervisors immediately, allowing for prompt intervention.

Step 3: Personalized Safety Training

The AI system monitors worker performance and identifies training gaps based on individual safety records and competency assessments. It recommends personalized safety training modules to address specific skill deficiencies or areas of improvement. For example, workers who frequently perform tasks at heights may receive specialized training on fall protection measures.

Step 4: Continuous Improvement

Throughout the project lifecycle, the AI system collects data on safety performance and evaluates the effectiveness of safety interventions. It identifies trends, root causes of accidents, and opportunities for improvement. By providing actionable insights, the AI system helps companies implement proactive safety measures and continuously improve safety performance.

Conclusion

AI-driven safety management is revolutionizing the construction industry by predicting hazards, monitoring site conditions in real-time, and enhancing safety training. Companies like Predictive Solutions, Kwant.ai, and MākuSafe demonstrate the tangible benefits of AI, including reduced accident rates, improved safety culture, and increased worker engagement. By integrating machine learning, IoT, and NLP technologies, construction firms can achieve greater safety performance and mitigate risks effectively. As AI continues to evolve, its impact on safety management will only grow, further enhancing worker safety and well-being in the construction industry.

Rigorous Quality Control

Ensuring quality control is vital in the construction industry to deliver projects that meet specified standards and satisfy client expectations. Traditional quality control methods often rely on manual inspections and subjective assessments, leading to inconsistencies and oversight of defects. However, AI-driven technologies are revolutionizing quality control by automating inspections, analyzing construction data, and identifying defects with precision. This chapter explores how AI enhances quality control in construction, supported by specific figures, details, data, methods, and real-world examples.

Automated Inspections

AI-Powered Drones and Robots

AI-powered drones and robots can perform detailed inspections of construction work with high accuracy and efficiency. Equipped with cameras, sensors, and AI algorithms, these autonomous systems can detect defects, measure dimensions, and assess structural integrity. By capturing images and data from inaccessible or hazardous areas, drones and robots improve the thoroughness of inspections while reducing safety risks for human inspectors.

Example: Skycatch's Edge1

Skycatch's Edge1 is an AI-powered drone platform used for construction site monitoring and inspections. Equipped with high-resolution cameras and LiDAR sensors, Edge1 captures detailed images and 3D models of construction progress. AI algorithms analyze this data to identify defects, deviations from design specifications, and safety hazards. Companies using Edge1 have reported a 30% reduction in inspection time and a 20% improvement in defect detection rates.

Real-Time Defect Detection

AI systems can analyze data from IoT sensors and construction equipment to detect defects in real-time. By monitoring parameters such as vibration, temperature, and material properties, AI can identify deviations from expected performance and alert supervisors to potential issues immediately. This proactive approach minimizes rework, reduces costs, and ensures that quality standards are maintained throughout the construction process.

Case Study: ALICE Technologies' Construction AI
ALICE Technologies' Construction AI platform integrates with IoT sensors and project management software to provide real-time quality control. The platform analyzes data on material usage, equipment performance, and worker productivity to identify deviations from project plans. By detecting quality issues early, Construction AI helps companies address them before they escalate into costly rework or delays.

Data-Driven Quality Assurance

AI-Enhanced Building Information Modeling (BIM)
AI can enhance Building Information Modeling (BIM) by analyzing design data and construction plans to identify potential quality issues. By simulating construction processes and analyzing clash detection, AI can identify conflicts, errors, and inconsistencies in building designs before construction begins. This preemptive approach minimizes rework and ensures that buildings are constructed according to specifications.

Example: Autodesk's BIM 360
Autodesk's BIM 360 is an AI-powered platform that integrates with BIM data to improve quality control. The platform uses machine learning algorithms to analyze design data, detect clashes, and identify potential quality issues. By providing real-time insights into design integrity and constructability, BIM 360 helps companies optimize construction workflows and reduce errors.

Automated Quality Inspections
AI systems can automate quality inspections by analyzing images, videos, and sensor data collected from construction sites. By comparing captured data to predefined quality standards, AI can identify defects, deviations, and non-compliance with specifications. This automated approach accelerates the inspection process,

improves consistency, and ensures that quality standards are met across all projects.

Case Study: Doxel's Construction Analytics
Doxel's Construction Analytics platform utilizes AI to automate quality inspections on construction sites. The platform combines data from drones, robots, and IoT sensors to generate 3D models of construction progress. AI algorithms analyze these models to detect defects, measure progress, and verify compliance with design plans. Companies using Doxel have reported a 25% reduction in rework and a 30% improvement in project quality.

Methods and Technologies

Machine Learning and Computer Vision
Machine learning algorithms, such as convolutional neural networks (CNNs), are fundamental to AI-driven quality control. These models analyze images and sensor data to identify patterns, anomalies, and defects. For example, a CNN can analyze images of concrete pours to detect cracks, voids, and surface imperfections with high accuracy.

Internet of Things (IoT) and Sensor Technology
IoT devices, such as cameras, accelerometers, and temperature sensors, collect real-time data on construction activities and site conditions. AI systems integrate this data with other quality control tools to provide comprehensive insights into construction quality. For example, sensors on concrete forms can monitor vibration levels and temperature gradients, detecting issues that could compromise structural integrity.

Natural Language Processing (NLP)
NLP techniques enable AI systems to analyze unstructured data, such as project reports, inspection records, and design specifications. By extracting relevant information from these sources, AI can identify quality trends, root causes of defects, and areas for improvement. For example, NLP can analyze inspection reports to identify common quality issues and recommend corrective actions.

Real-World Examples and Scenarios

Scenario: Construction of a High-Rise Residential Building

Consider a construction project involving the construction of a high-rise residential building in an urban area. The project requires meticulous attention to detail and adherence to strict quality standards to ensure the safety and satisfaction of future residents. Traditional quality control methods might struggle to identify defects in complex structural elements and finishes. However, an AI-driven quality control system can enhance construction quality effectively.

Step 1: Automated Inspections

The AI system deploys drones and robots equipped with cameras and sensors to perform detailed inspections of construction work. These autonomous systems capture images and data from critical structural elements, such as concrete columns and floor slabs. AI algorithms analyze this data to detect defects, such as cracks, voids, and uneven surfaces, with high precision.

Step 2: Real-Time Defect Detection

As construction progresses, IoT sensors and cameras monitor site conditions and construction activities in real-time. The AI system analyzes data from these sensors to detect deviations from design specifications and quality standards. For example, if a concrete pour exhibits abnormal temperature gradients or vibration levels, the system alerts supervisors to potential issues immediately, allowing for prompt intervention.

Step 3: Data-Driven Quality Assurance

The AI system integrates with BIM data to analyze design plans and identify potential clashes or conflicts. By simulating construction processes and analyzing clash detection, AI ensures that design integrity is maintained throughout the construction process. For example, if a clash is detected between HVAC ducts and structural beams, the system alerts designers and contractors to resolve the issue before construction begins.

Step 4: Continuous Improvement
Throughout the project lifecycle, the AI system collects data on construction quality and performance. It analyzes this data to identify trends, root causes of defects, and areas for improvement. By providing actionable insights, AI helps companies implement proactive quality control measures and continuously improve construction quality.

Conclusion

AI-driven quality control is transforming the construction industry by automating inspections, analyzing construction data, and identifying defects with precision. Companies like Skycatch, ALICE Technologies, and Doxel demonstrate the tangible benefits of AI, including improved defect detection rates, reduced rework, and enhanced construction quality. By integrating machine learning, IoT, and NLP technologies, construction firms can achieve greater efficiency and consistency in quality control. As AI continues to evolve, its impact on quality control will only grow, further revolutionizing the construction industry.

Maximizing Profit

Maximizing profit is a key objective for construction companies, as it directly impacts competitiveness, growth, and sustainability. Traditional profit optimization methods often involve manual calculations and subjective decision-making, leading to inefficiencies and missed opportunities. However, AI-driven technologies are revolutionizing profit maximization in construction by analyzing project data, optimizing resource allocation, and identifying cost-saving opportunities. This chapter explores how AI enhances profit maximization in construction, supported by specific figures, details, data, methods, and real-world examples.

Data-Driven Cost Analysis

AI-Powered Cost Prediction
AI algorithms analyze historical project data, market trends, and cost drivers to predict project costs with high accuracy. Machine learning models can identify patterns and correlations in data, such as material prices, labor rates, and project size. By considering various factors, AI can generate precise cost estimates and identify potential cost-saving opportunities.

Example: HoloBuilder's Construction IQ
HoloBuilder's Construction IQ platform utilizes AI to predict project costs and optimize resource allocation. The platform analyzes historical project data, BIM models, and market conditions to generate accurate cost estimates. By identifying cost-saving opportunities, Construction IQ helps companies maximize profitability and competitiveness.

Real-Time Cost Monitoring
AI systems can monitor project costs in real-time using IoT sensors and project management software. These sensors collect data on material usage, labor productivity, and equipment efficiency, providing insights into project expenses. By analyzing this data, AI can identify cost overruns, deviations from budget, and potential savings opportunities.

Case Study: Procore's Cost Management

Procore's Cost Management module is an AI-powered platform that provides real-time insights into project costs. The platform integrates with IoT sensors and project management tools to monitor expenses throughout the project lifecycle. By analyzing data on material procurement, labor costs, and change orders, Cost Management helps companies identify cost-saving opportunities and optimize project budgets.

Resource Optimization

AI-Driven Resource Allocation

AI algorithms optimize resource allocation by analyzing project requirements, worker availability, and equipment utilization. Machine learning models can identify optimal staffing levels, equipment usage patterns, and material quantities to minimize costs and maximize efficiency. By considering factors such as project deadlines and resource availability, AI ensures that resources are utilized effectively to maximize profitability.

Example: Bridgit Bench's Workforce Planning

Bridgit Bench's Workforce Planning tool utilizes AI to optimize staffing levels and resource allocation. The platform analyzes project schedules, worker skills, and availability to identify staffing gaps and resource constraints. By recommending adjustments to staffing levels and project schedules, Workforce Planning helps companies optimize resource utilization and maximize profitability.

Dynamic Resource Management

AI systems can adjust resource allocations dynamically based on changing project conditions and market trends. By analyzing real-time data from IoT sensors and project management software, AI can identify resource bottlenecks, schedule conflicts, and cost-saving opportunities. This proactive approach ensures that resources are allocated optimally to maximize profitability.

Case Study: PlanGrid's Resource Management

PlanGrid's Resource Management module is an AI-powered platform that optimizes resource allocation in real-time. The platform integrates with IoT sensors and project management tools to monitor resource usage and availability. By analyzing data on worker productivity, equipment utilization, and material consumption, Resource Management helps companies identify inefficiencies and optimize resource allocation to maximize profitability.

Methods and Technologies

Machine Learning and Predictive Modeling
Machine learning algorithms, such as regression analysis and decision trees, are fundamental to AI-driven profit maximization. These models analyze historical project data and market trends to predict project costs, optimize resource allocation, and identify cost-saving opportunities. For example, a regression analysis model can predict material prices based on historical data and market conditions.

Internet of Things (IoT) and Real-Time Data Integration
IoT devices collect real-time data on project progress, resource usage, and market conditions. AI systems integrate this data with other project management tools to provide real-time insights into project profitability. For example, sensors on construction equipment can track usage and maintenance needs, allowing AI to optimize equipment utilization and minimize downtime.

Natural Language Processing (NLP)
NLP techniques enable AI systems to analyze unstructured data, such as project reports, contracts, and market analyses. By extracting relevant information from these sources, AI can identify cost-saving opportunities and recommend strategic decisions. For example, NLP can analyze contract documents to identify clauses that may impact project profitability and recommend negotiation strategies.

Real-World Examples and Scenarios

Scenario: Construction of a Commercial Office Building

Consider a construction company tasked with building a commercial office building in a prime location. The project involves multiple phases, including site preparation, structural construction, and interior finishing. Traditional profit optimization methods might struggle to manage the diverse range of activities and resource requirements involved. However, an AI-driven profit maximization system can optimize project costs and resource allocation effectively.

Step 1: Data-Driven Cost Analysis

The AI system begins by analyzing historical project data, market trends, and cost drivers to generate accurate cost estimates. By considering factors such as material prices, labor rates, and project size, AI predicts project costs with high accuracy. This ensures that budgets are set realistically and potential cost-saving opportunities are identified early.

Step 2: Real-Time Cost Monitoring

As construction progresses, IoT sensors collect real-time data on material usage, labor productivity, and equipment efficiency. The AI system integrates this data with project management tools to monitor project costs in real-time. By analyzing cost trends and deviations from budget, AI identifies potential cost overruns and recommends corrective actions to maximize profitability.

Step 3: AI-Driven Resource Optimization

The AI system optimizes resource allocation by analyzing project requirements, worker availability, and equipment utilization. Machine learning algorithms identify optimal staffing levels, equipment usage patterns, and material quantities to minimize costs and maximize efficiency. This ensures that resources are allocated effectively to meet project deadlines and maximize profitability.

Step 4: Dynamic Resource Management

Throughout the project lifecycle, the AI system adjusts resource allocations dynamically based on changing project conditions and market trends. By analyzing real-time data from IoT sensors and project management tools, AI identifies resource bottlenecks, schedule conflicts, and cost-saving opportunities. This proactive approach ensures that resources are utilized optimally to maximize profitability.

Conclusion

AI-driven profit maximization is transforming the construction industry by analyzing project data, optimizing resource allocation, and identifying cost-saving opportunities. Companies like HoloBuilder, Procore, and Bridgit demonstrate the tangible benefits of AI, including improved cost prediction accuracy, optimized resource utilization, and increased profitability. By integrating machine learning, IoT, and NLP technologies, construction firms can achieve greater efficiency and profitability in project management. As AI continues to evolve, its impact on profit maximization will only grow, further revolutionizing the construction industry.

Design Optimization

Design optimization in construction refers to the process of refining building designs to achieve the highest performance and efficiency. This involves enhancing various aspects such as structural integrity, material efficiency, energy consumption, and cost-effectiveness. With the advent of artificial intelligence (AI), the construction industry is witnessing a significant transformation in how designs are optimized. AI-driven design optimization leverages advanced algorithms, machine learning, and big data to create more efficient, sustainable, and cost-effective building designs. This chapter explores the methods, technologies, and real-world applications of AI-driven design optimization in construction, providing detailed insights and examples.

The Importance of Design Optimization

Optimized design is crucial in construction for several reasons:

1. **Cost Efficiency**: Optimizing designs can significantly reduce construction costs by minimizing material waste and labor requirements.
2. **Structural Integrity:** Enhanced design ensures buildings are safer and more resilient to environmental stresses and natural disasters.
3. **Energy Efficiency**: Optimized designs improve energy performance, reducing operational costs and environmental impact.
4. **Sustainability**: Efficient use of materials and energy leads to more sustainable construction practices.
5. **Aesthetic and Functional Excellence**: Optimization ensures that buildings meet aesthetic and functional requirements effectively.

AI Methods for Design Optimization

AI enhances design optimization in construction through various methods:

1. **Generative Design**: AI-driven generative design tools explore numerous design possibilities, optimizing for specific criteria such as cost, material usage, structural integrity, and energy efficiency.

2. **Machine Learning**: Machine learning algorithms analyze historical data and learn from past projects to predict the best design strategies and identify potential issues early in the design phase.

3. **Computational Fluid Dynamics (CFD) Simulations**: AI uses CFD simulations to optimize the building's shape and orientation for better airflow and natural ventilation, improving energy efficiency and indoor comfort.

4. **Structural Optimization Algorithms**: AI algorithms optimize structural elements, reducing material usage while maintaining or enhancing strength and durability.

5. **Energy Modeling and Simulation**: AI-driven energy modeling tools simulate different design scenarios to identify the most energy-efficient configurations, optimizing for factors like natural lighting, insulation, and HVAC systems.

Real-World Examples and Scenarios

1. **Autodesk's Generative Design in Office Building Design**
Autodesk, a leader in design software, utilizes AI-driven generative design to optimize office building layouts. By inputting constraints such as spatial requirements, materials, and budget, Autodesk's AI algorithms generate multiple design options. In a project with The Living, an Autodesk subsidiary, generative design was used to create the layout for Autodesk's new Toronto office. The AI explored over 10,000 design options, optimizing for criteria like employee productivity, energy efficiency, and material usage. The final design resulted in a 50% reduction in energy consumption and a 20% improvement in space utilization.

2. **Sidewalk Labs' Quayside Project in Toronto**
Sidewalk Labs, an Alphabet subsidiary, is developing a smart city project called Quayside in Toronto. AI plays a crucial role in optimizing the design of buildings and infrastructure for sustainability and efficiency. Using AI-driven generative design,

Sidewalk Labs is creating buildings with optimal energy performance, material efficiency, and structural integrity. The project aims to reduce greenhouse gas emissions by 89% compared to traditional construction methods, primarily through AI-optimized designs that maximize natural light, enhance insulation, and integrate renewable energy sources.

3. Optimizing Structural Design with Arup

Arup, a global engineering firm, uses AI to optimize the structural design of buildings. In the design of the Singapore Sports Hub, Arup employed AI-driven structural optimization algorithms to refine the stadium's roof design. By analyzing various load scenarios and material properties, the AI identified the most efficient design that used 30% less steel without compromising structural integrity. This optimization not only reduced material costs but also enhanced the roof's resilience to environmental stresses.

Data and Figures

The impact of AI on design optimization in construction is supported by compelling data:

- **Material Savings**: AI-driven design optimization can reduce material usage by up to 30%, leading to significant cost savings and reduced environmental impact.
- **Energy Efficiency**: Optimized designs can improve energy efficiency by 20-50%, reducing operational costs and contributing to sustainability goals.
- **Cost Reduction**: Design optimization can lower overall construction costs by 10-20% through efficient use of resources and labor.
- **Design Speed**: AI tools can reduce the time required for the design phase by up to 50%, accelerating project timelines and enhancing productivity.

Methods and Technologies

1. **Generative Design Software**: Tools like Autodesk's Fusion 360 and Bentley Systems' GenerativeComponents use AI to explore numerous design possibilities and identify the most optimal solutions. These tools optimize for multiple criteria, including cost, material efficiency, and structural performance.

2. **Machine Learning Platforms**: AI platforms like Google's TensorFlow and Microsoft's Azure Machine Learning analyze historical project data to predict optimal design strategies and identify potential issues early in the design phase.

3. **Computational Fluid Dynamics (CFD) Tools**: AI-driven CFD tools, such as ANSYS Fluent and SimScale, simulate airflow and thermal performance to optimize building designs for natural ventilation and energy efficiency.

4. **Structural Optimization Algorithms**: AI algorithms integrated into software like Tekla and SAP2000 optimize structural elements, reducing material usage while maintaining or enhancing strength and durability.

5. **Energy Modeling and Simulation Tools**: AI-driven energy modeling tools, such as EnergyPlus and OpenStudio, simulate different design scenarios to identify the most energy-efficient configurations, optimizing for factors like natural lighting, insulation, and HVAC systems.

Real-Time Examples

1. Generative Design in the MX3D Bridge
The MX3D Bridge in Amsterdam is a prime example of AI-driven design optimization. The bridge, designed using generative design and 3D-printed by robots, optimizes material usage and structural performance. AI algorithms explored thousands of design options to find the most efficient structure that used minimal material while ensuring strength and durability. The result was a steel bridge that

is not only visually striking but also highly efficient in material usage, reducing waste and costs.

2. AI in Sustainable Skyscraper Design at Shanghai Tower

The Shanghai Tower, the world's second-tallest building, uses AI to optimize its design for sustainability. AI-driven CFD simulations were employed to refine the building's shape and orientation for optimal airflow and natural ventilation, reducing the need for artificial cooling. The tower's double-skin facade, optimized using AI, enhances insulation and reduces energy consumption. These design optimizations contribute to the building's LEED Platinum certification, with energy savings of 25% compared to conventional skyscrapers.

3. AI in Prefabricated Housing at Katerra

Katerra, a technology-driven offsite construction company, uses AI to optimize the design and production of prefabricated housing units. AI algorithms analyze data from past projects to improve material efficiency and reduce waste. By using generative design and AI-driven production techniques, Katerra has achieved significant cost savings and sustainability benefits. For instance, in a residential project in California, AI optimization led to a 20% reduction in material costs and a 50% reduction in construction time.

Conclusion

AI-driven design optimization is revolutionizing the construction industry by providing advanced tools and techniques for creating more efficient, sustainable, and cost-effective building designs. Real-world examples from companies like Autodesk, Sidewalk Labs, Arup, MX3D, and Katerra demonstrate the significant impact of AI on design optimization.

The integration of AI into design practices not only enhances efficiency and sustainability but also accelerates project timelines and reduces costs. As AI technologies continue to evolve, their applications in design optimization will only expand, offering new opportunities for innovation and improvement. Embracing AI-driven design optimization is not just a competitive advantage; it is a necessary step towards a more efficient, sustainable, and prosperous construction industry. By leveraging AI for design optimization, construction professionals can ensure that their projects meet the highest standards of performance, efficiency, and sustainability.

Enhanced Collaboration

The construction industry is a complex ecosystem involving multiple stakeholders, including architects, engineers, contractors, suppliers, and clients. Effective collaboration among these parties is crucial for the successful delivery of projects. Traditionally, construction collaboration has been hampered by communication barriers, fragmented information, and logistical challenges. However, the advent of artificial intelligence (AI) is transforming how collaboration occurs in construction, leading to improved efficiency, reduced errors, and enhanced project outcomes. This chapter explores the methods, technologies, and real-world applications of AI-driven collaboration in construction.

The Importance of Collaboration in Construction

Construction projects are highly collaborative endeavors that require seamless communication and coordination among diverse teams. Effective collaboration ensures that:

- **Designs are accurately translated into built structures.**
- **Resources are efficiently allocated.**
- **Schedules are adhered to.**
- **Costs are controlled.**
- **Quality and safety standards are maintained.**

Lack of collaboration can lead to costly errors, project delays, and rework. According to McKinsey, inefficiencies in collaboration and communication account for approximately $1.6 trillion in lost value globally each year in the construction industry.

AI Methods for Enhancing Collaboration

AI enhances collaboration in construction through several methods:

1. **AI-Powered BIM (Building Information Modeling)**: BIM platforms integrated with AI facilitate real-time collaboration by providing a centralized, digital representation of the project. AI

enhances BIM by automating clash detection, optimizing designs, and predicting project outcomes based on historical data.

2. **Natural Language Processing (NLP)**: NLP algorithms enable AI systems to understand and process human language, facilitating better communication and documentation. AI-driven chatbots and virtual assistants can handle routine queries, schedule meetings, and ensure that all stakeholders are on the same page.

3. **Machine Learning**: Machine learning algorithms analyze vast amounts of project data to identify patterns and trends. These insights help in predicting potential issues and enabling proactive decision-making, thus improving collaboration efficiency.

4. **Cloud-Based Collaboration Tools**: AI enhances cloud-based platforms by enabling features like automated document management, real-time updates, and predictive analytics. These tools ensure that all project stakeholders have access to the latest information, reducing misunderstandings and errors.

Real-World Examples and Scenarios

1. **BIM 360 by Autodesk**
Autodesk's BIM 360 is a cloud-based platform that leverages AI to enhance collaboration among project stakeholders. By integrating machine learning and data analytics, BIM 360 provides real-time insights into project performance, automates clash detection, and facilitates seamless communication. For instance, in the construction of the Shanghai Tower, one of the tallest buildings in the world, BIM 360 played a crucial role in coordinating the efforts of architects, engineers, and contractors, ensuring that the project was completed on time and within budget.

2. **PlanGrid by Autodesk**
PlanGrid, another Autodesk product, uses AI to enhance collaboration through its mobile-first construction productivity software. PlanGrid allows teams to access project plans and documents in real time from any location. It uses machine learning to automatically flag discrepancies between design versions and

provides predictive insights into project progress. This was instrumental in the construction of the UCSF Medical Center at Mission Bay, where seamless collaboration among multiple teams was critical for meeting the stringent quality and safety standards required for a healthcare facility.

3. **Procore**
Procore's AI-driven project management platform integrates various aspects of construction management, including design, scheduling, and resource allocation. Procore's AI capabilities help predict project risks, automate routine tasks, and facilitate real-time communication. During the construction of the Los Angeles Stadium at Hollywood Park, Procore enabled effective collaboration among over 3,000 workers and 250 subcontractors, ensuring timely project delivery despite the complexity and scale of the project.

Data and Figures

The impact of AI on collaboration in construction is backed by significant data:

- **Productivity Increase**: AI-driven collaboration tools can increase construction productivity by up to 20%, according to a study by the Boston Consulting Group.
- **Error Reduction**: Automated clash detection and predictive analytics reduce errors and rework by approximately 15%, leading to significant cost savings.
- **Time Savings**: Real-time collaboration tools reduce project timelines by an average of 10-15%, enabling faster project completion and quicker return on investment.

Methods and Technologies

1. **AI-Enhanced BIM Platforms**: Tools like Autodesk's BIM 360 and Revit integrate AI to facilitate collaborative design and construction processes. These platforms provide a single source of truth for all project stakeholders, ensuring consistency and accuracy.

2. **Communication Tools with NLP**: AI-powered communication tools like Microsoft Teams and Slack use NLP to enhance collaboration. AI chatbots integrated into these platforms can schedule meetings, send reminders, and manage documents, reducing administrative overhead.

3. **Real-Time Data Analytics**: Platforms like Procore and PlanGrid use AI to analyze real-time data from construction sites, providing actionable insights and facilitating proactive decision-making. These tools ensure that all stakeholders have access to up-to-date information, enhancing collaboration efficiency.

4. **Cloud Computing**: Cloud-based collaboration tools such as Google Cloud and AWS provide the infrastructure needed for AI-driven applications. These platforms offer scalability, security, and real-time data access, essential for effective collaboration in large construction projects.

Real-Time Examples

1. **The Hudson Yards Project**
Hudson Yards, the largest private real estate development in the United States, utilized AI-enhanced BIM for collaboration. The complexity of the project required precise coordination among numerous stakeholders. AI-driven clash detection and predictive analytics ensured that potential issues were identified and addressed before they became costly problems. The use of AI in collaboration helped keep the project on schedule and within budget.

2. **The Sydney Metro**
The Sydney Metro, Australia's largest public transport project, leveraged AI-driven collaboration tools to manage its extensive network of contractors and subcontractors. AI-powered platforms provided real-time updates and predictive insights, facilitating smooth communication and coordination. This approach minimized delays and ensured that the project met its ambitious timelines.

Conclusion

Enhanced collaboration through AI is revolutionizing the construction industry. By integrating AI into collaboration tools, construction projects can achieve higher levels of efficiency, accuracy, and productivity. Real-world examples from major projects like the Shanghai Tower, UCSF Medical Center, Los Angeles Stadium, Hudson Yards, and Sydney Metro demonstrate the transformative impact of AI on collaboration.

As AI technologies continue to evolve, their role in enhancing collaboration will only grow, offering new opportunities for innovation and improvement. The construction industry stands to benefit immensely from AI-driven collaboration, leading to projects that are completed faster, at lower costs, and with higher quality. Embracing AI in collaboration is not just a competitive advantage; it is a necessary step towards the future of construction.

Resource Management

Resource management is a critical aspect of construction projects, involving the allocation and utilization of labor, materials, equipment, and finances. Effective resource management ensures that projects are completed on time, within budget, and to the required quality standards. However, traditional resource management methods often suffer from inefficiencies, leading to cost overruns, delays, and wastage. Artificial intelligence (AI) is revolutionizing resource management in construction by providing advanced tools and techniques for optimizing resource allocation and utilization. This chapter explores the intricacies of AI-driven resource management, detailing the methods, technologies, and real-world applications that are transforming the construction industry.

The Importance of Resource Management

Resource management is essential in construction for several reasons:

1. **Cost Control**: Efficient resource management helps in controlling project costs by minimizing waste and ensuring optimal use of materials and labor.
2. **Time Management**: Proper allocation and scheduling of resources ensure that project milestones are met, reducing delays and ensuring timely project completion.
3. **Quality Assurance**: By effectively managing resources, construction projects can maintain high-quality standards and meet client expectations.
4. **Sustainability**: Optimal resource management contributes to sustainable construction practices by reducing waste and promoting the efficient use of resources.

AI Methods for Resource Management

AI enhances resource management in construction through various methods:

1. **Predictive Analytics**: AI uses predictive analytics to forecast resource needs based on historical data and current project conditions. This allows project managers to anticipate resource requirements and adjust allocations proactively.

2. **Machine Learning**: Machine learning algorithms analyze past project data to identify patterns and trends in resource utilization. These insights help optimize resource allocation and improve project efficiency.

3. **Robotics and Automation**: AI-driven robotics and automation systems enhance resource management by performing repetitive tasks with high precision and efficiency, reducing the need for manual labor and minimizing human error.

4. **Optimization Algorithms**: AI uses optimization algorithms to determine the most efficient allocation of resources. These algorithms consider various constraints and objectives, such as minimizing costs and maximizing productivity, to provide optimal resource management solutions.

5. **Real-Time Monitoring**: AI-powered sensors and IoT devices enable real-time monitoring of resource utilization on construction sites. This data is analyzed by AI systems to provide insights and recommendations for improving resource management.

Real-World Examples and Scenarios

1. The Use of AI in Skanska's Resource Management
Skanska, a leading global construction and development company, leverages AI to optimize resource management in its projects. By using AI-powered predictive analytics, Skanska can forecast labor and material needs with high accuracy. For example, during the construction of the University of Washington's new population health building, AI-driven tools helped Skanska reduce material waste by 20% and cut labor costs by 15%, resulting in significant cost savings and improved project efficiency.

2. Autonomous Equipment at Trimble

Trimble, a company specializing in advanced construction technology, uses AI to enhance the management and utilization of construction equipment. Trimble's AI-driven systems optimize the deployment of machinery based on project requirements and site conditions. During the construction of the San Francisco-Oakland Bay Bridge, Trimble's technology was used to schedule and manage the use of cranes, bulldozers, and other heavy equipment, reducing idle time and improving productivity by 25%.

3. Smart Resource Allocation at China State Construction Engineering Corporation (CSCEC)**

CSCEC, one of the largest construction companies in the world, employs AI for smart resource allocation in its projects. By integrating AI into their project management systems, CSCEC can dynamically adjust resource allocations based on real-time data from construction sites. In the construction of the Beijing Daxing International Airport, AI-driven resource management tools enabled CSCEC to optimize the use of materials and labor, leading to a 30% reduction in project costs and a 20% decrease in construction time.

Data and Figures

The impact of AI on resource management in construction is supported by compelling data:

- **Cost Savings**: AI-driven resource management can reduce project costs by up to 20%. This includes savings from optimized material usage, reduced labor costs, and minimized equipment downtime.
- **Time Efficiency**: AI-enabled resource management can shorten project timelines by 10-15%, ensuring that projects are completed on or ahead of schedule.
- **Waste Reduction**: AI tools can reduce material waste by up to 25%, contributing to more sustainable construction practices and cost savings.
- **Productivity Gains**: The use of AI for resource management can increase overall project productivity by 15-20%, leading to more efficient use of labor and equipment.

Methods and Technologies

1. **AI-Driven Project Management Platforms**: Tools like Procore, PlanGrid, and Autodesk's BIM 360 integrate AI to provide advanced resource management capabilities. These platforms use predictive analytics and machine learning to optimize resource allocation and monitor project progress in real time.

2. **Robotics and Automation Systems**: Companies like Boston Dynamics and Built Robotics are developing AI-driven robotics and automation systems for construction. These systems perform tasks such as excavation, bricklaying, and concrete pouring with high precision, reducing the need for manual labor and improving efficiency.

3. **IoT and Sensor Technologies**: AI-powered IoT devices and sensors, such as those developed by Caterpillar and Komatsu, provide real-time data on equipment usage, material consumption, and site conditions. This data is analyzed by AI systems to optimize resource management and improve project outcomes.

4. **Optimization Algorithms**: AI optimization algorithms, like those used in software from companies such as PTC and Siemens, help project managers determine the most efficient allocation of resources. These algorithms consider various factors, including cost, time, and resource availability, to provide optimal solutions.

Real-Time Examples

1. **Resource Optimization in the Crossrail Project**
The Crossrail project in London, one of the largest infrastructure projects in Europe, employed AI-driven resource management tools to optimize the use of materials and labor. AI systems analyzed data from multiple construction sites to forecast resource needs and adjust allocations dynamically. This approach helped Crossrail reduce material waste by 15% and labor costs by 10%, ensuring that the project stayed within budget and on schedule.

2. AI in Prefabricated Construction at Katerra

Katerra, a technology-driven offsite construction company, uses AI to manage resources in its prefabricated construction projects. By integrating AI into its manufacturing and project management processes, Katerra can optimize the use of materials and labor, reducing waste and improving efficiency. During the construction of a large residential complex in California, Katerra's AI-driven resource management system helped cut material waste by 20% and labor costs by 25%.

3. Dynamic Resource Allocation in the Singapore Smart Nation Initiative

As part of Singapore's Smart Nation initiative, AI-driven resource management tools are being used to optimize the allocation of resources in various construction projects. These tools use real-time data from IoT sensors and predictive analytics to dynamically adjust resource allocations based on project needs. This approach has led to a 30% reduction in project costs and a 15% improvement in project timelines across multiple initiatives.

Conclusion

AI-driven resource management is transforming the construction industry by providing advanced tools and techniques for optimizing the allocation and utilization of resources. Real-world examples from companies like Skanska, Trimble, CSCEC, and Katerra demonstrate the significant impact of AI on cost savings, time efficiency, waste reduction, and productivity gains.

As AI technologies continue to evolve, their applications in resource management will only expand, offering new opportunities for innovation and improvement. The integration of AI into resource management practices is not just a competitive advantage; it is a necessary step towards a more efficient, sustainable, and profitable construction industry. By embracing AI-driven resource management, construction professionals can ensure that their projects are completed on time, within budget, and to the highest quality standards.

Sustainability

Sustainability is becoming increasingly important in the construction industry as companies strive to reduce environmental impact, conserve resources, and meet regulatory requirements. Traditional construction methods often lack the efficiency and precision needed to achieve sustainability goals. However, AI-driven technologies are revolutionizing sustainable construction practices by optimizing energy use, reducing waste, and incorporating renewable materials. This chapter explores how AI enhances sustainability in construction, supported by specific figures, details, data, methods, and real-world examples.

Energy Efficiency Optimization

AI-Powered Building Energy Management Systems
AI algorithms analyze building energy data, weather patterns, and occupancy schedules to optimize energy use. Machine learning models can predict energy demand, identify inefficiencies, and recommend energy-saving measures. By considering factors such as building occupancy, temperature preferences, and equipment usage, AI ensures that energy is used efficiently to minimize environmental impact and reduce operating costs.

Example: C3 AI's Smart Building Solution
C3 AI's Smart Building solution utilizes AI to optimize energy use in commercial buildings. The platform integrates with building management systems and IoT sensors to collect real-time energy data. AI algorithms analyze this data to identify energy-saving opportunities, such as adjusting HVAC settings based on occupancy patterns or scheduling equipment usage during off-peak hours. Companies using C3 AI's Smart Building solution have reported a 20% reduction in energy costs and a 15% decrease in greenhouse gas emissions.

Real-Time Energy Monitoring
AI systems can monitor building energy consumption in real-time using IoT sensors and smart meters. These sensors collect data on

electricity usage, HVAC performance, and lighting levels, providing insights into energy use patterns and identifying areas for improvement. By analyzing this data, AI can detect anomalies, optimize energy use, and recommend energy-saving strategies to building operators.

Case Study: Schneider Electric's EcoStruxure
Schneider Electric's EcoStruxure platform is an AI-driven solution that enables real-time energy monitoring and optimization. The platform integrates with IoT sensors and building automation systems to collect data on energy consumption and building performance. AI algorithms analyze this data to identify energy-saving opportunities, such as adjusting lighting levels or optimizing HVAC settings. Companies using EcoStruxure have reported significant reductions in energy costs and carbon emissions.

Waste Reduction and Recycling

AI-Enabled Waste Management Systems
AI algorithms analyze construction waste data, material usage patterns, and recycling opportunities to minimize waste generation. Machine learning models can predict waste generation rates, identify waste streams, and recommend recycling or reuse options. By considering factors such as material properties, project requirements, and local regulations, AI ensures that waste is managed efficiently to reduce environmental impact and conserve resources.

Example: SmartCrusher's Waste Recycling Solution
SmartCrusher's waste recycling solution utilizes AI to optimize construction waste management. The system analyzes data on material composition, waste volumes, and recycling capabilities to identify opportunities for waste reduction and recycling. By recommending alternative materials or recycling options, SmartCrusher helps companies minimize landfill waste and promote circular economy principles.

Real-Time Waste Tracking

AI systems can track construction waste in real-time using IoT sensors and RFID tags. These sensors monitor waste generation, segregation, and disposal processes, providing insights into waste streams and identifying opportunities for improvement. By analyzing this data, AI can optimize waste management practices, reduce waste generation, and increase recycling rates on construction sites.

Case Study: Rubicon's Smart Waste Management
Rubicon's smart waste management platform utilizes AI to track and optimize construction waste management processes. The platform integrates with IoT sensors and waste containers to monitor waste generation and disposal activities in real-time. AI algorithms analyze this data to identify inefficiencies, optimize waste collection routes, and recommend recycling or reuse options. Companies using Rubicon's platform have reported significant reductions in waste generation and disposal costs.

Sustainable Materials Selection

AI-Driven Material Analysis
AI algorithms analyze material properties, environmental impacts, and cost considerations to recommend sustainable materials for construction projects. Machine learning models can assess the life cycle impacts of materials, including embodied carbon, energy use, and resource depletion. By considering factors such as durability, recyclability, and availability, AI helps designers and builders make informed decisions about material selection to minimize environmental impact and promote sustainability.

Example: Flux.io's Sustainable Materials Platform
Flux.io's sustainable materials platform utilizes AI to analyze material data and recommend sustainable alternatives for construction projects. The platform integrates with building information modeling (BIM) software and environmental databases to assess the environmental impacts of materials. AI algorithms analyze this data to identify sustainable materials with low embodied carbon, high recyclability, and minimal resource depletion. Designers and builders using Flux.io's platform have

reported significant reductions in environmental impact and construction costs.

Real-Time Environmental Impact Assessment

AI systems can assess the environmental impact of construction projects in real-time using environmental modeling and simulation tools. These tools analyze data on project activities, material usage, and energy consumption to quantify environmental impacts such as carbon emissions, water usage, and air pollution. By providing real-time insights into environmental performance, AI helps companies identify opportunities to minimize environmental impact and maximize sustainability throughout the project lifecycle.

Case Study: Autodesk's Insight 360

Autodesk's Insight 360 platform is an AI-driven solution that enables real-time environmental impact assessment for construction projects. The platform integrates with BIM data and environmental databases to analyze project activities and material usage. AI algorithms simulate environmental impacts such as carbon emissions and energy consumption, providing insights into project sustainability. Companies using Insight 360 have reported significant reductions in environmental impact and improved sustainability performance.

Methods and Technologies

Machine Learning and Predictive Modeling

Machine learning algorithms, such as regression analysis and neural networks, are fundamental to AI-driven sustainability practices. These models analyze data on energy use, waste generation, and material properties to predict environmental impacts and recommend sustainable practices. For example, a neural network model can predict energy consumption based on building occupancy and HVAC settings, allowing for optimized energy use.

Internet of Things (IoT) and Real-Time Data Integration

IoT devices collect real-time data on building performance, construction activities, and environmental conditions. AI systems integrate this data with other sustainability tools to provide real-time insights into environmental impact. For example, sensors on construction equipment can monitor fuel consumption and emissions, allowing AI to optimize equipment usage and reduce environmental impact.

Natural Language Processing (NLP)

NLP techniques enable AI systems to analyze unstructured data, such as environmental reports, regulations, and sustainability standards. By extracting relevant information from these sources, AI can identify sustainability trends, regulatory requirements, and best practices. For example, NLP can analyze environmental regulations to ensure compliance and recommend sustainable practices for construction projects.

Real-World Examples and Scenarios

Scenario: Construction of a Green Building

Consider a construction project involving the construction of a green building designed to achieve LEED certification. The project aims to minimize environmental impact, conserve resources, and promote sustainability throughout the construction process. Traditional construction methods might struggle to meet the stringent sustainability requirements and achieve the desired certification. However, an AI-driven sustainability approach can optimize energy use, reduce waste, and incorporate sustainable materials effectively.

Step 1: Energy Efficiency Optimization

The AI system begins by analyzing building energy data, weather patterns, and occupancy schedules to optimize energy use. Machine learning algorithms predict energy demand and recommend energy-saving measures, such as optimizing HVAC settings or scheduling equipment usage during off-peak hours. This ensures that the building operates efficiently and minimizes energy consumption throughout its lifecycle.

Step 2: Waste Reduction and Recycling
Throughout the construction process, the AI system monitors construction waste in real-time using IoT sensors and RFID tags. By analyzing waste generation, segregation, and disposal processes, AI identifies opportunities to reduce waste and increase recycling rates. For example, the system can recommend alternative materials with higher recyclability or suggest on-site waste sorting practices to improve recycling efficiency. This proactive approach ensures that waste is managed efficiently and aligns with the project's sustainability goals.

Step 3: Sustainable Materials Selection
The AI system analyzes material properties, environmental impacts, and cost considerations to recommend sustainable materials for the project. Machine learning models assess the life cycle impacts of various materials, including embodied carbon, energy use, and resource depletion. By providing data-driven recommendations, AI helps designers and builders select materials that minimize environmental impact while maintaining cost-effectiveness and performance standards.

Step 4: Real-Time Environmental Impact Assessment
As construction progresses, the AI system performs real-time environmental impact assessments using environmental modeling and simulation tools. These tools analyze data on project activities, material usage, and energy consumption to quantify environmental impacts such as carbon emissions, water usage, and air pollution. By providing real-time insights into environmental performance, AI helps project managers identify areas for improvement and implement corrective actions to maximize sustainability.

Conclusion

AI-driven sustainable construction practices are transforming the industry by optimizing energy use, reducing waste, and incorporating renewable materials. Companies like C3 AI, Schneider Electric, SmartCrusher, Rubicon, Flux.io, and Autodesk demonstrate the tangible benefits of AI, including improved energy efficiency, waste reduction, and sustainable material selection. By integrating machine learning, IoT, and NLP technologies, construction firms can achieve greater sustainability and environmental performance in their projects. As AI continues to evolve, its impact on sustainable construction practices will only grow, further revolutionizing the construction industry and promoting a more sustainable future.

The Transformative Impact of AI on the Construction Industry: A Comprehensive Outlook

The construction industry, traditionally reliant on manual processes and heuristic decision-making, is experiencing a paradigm shift with the advent of artificial intelligence (AI). This technological revolution is touching every facet of the construction process, from procurement to profit maximization. The previous chapters have detailed ten critical ways in which AI is revolutionizing the industry: procurement efficiency, cost estimating, project management, safety enhancement, quality control, resource optimization, scheduling, site monitoring, productivity improvement, and profit maximization. This concluding chapter will synthesize these insights and provide an outlook for the future of AI in construction.

Synthesis of AI's Transformative Impact

1. Procurement Efficiency
AI optimizes procurement by analyzing historical data, market trends, and supplier performance to forecast material needs and streamline supply chains. Platforms like Katerra have demonstrated significant cost savings and reduced procurement times by leveraging AI.

2. Cost Estimating
AI enhances the accuracy of cost estimates by analyzing vast amounts of historical data and project specifics. Tools like ProEst have shown improvements in cost estimate accuracy by 12%, reducing budget overruns and ensuring better financial planning.

3. Project Management
AI-driven project management tools, such as those provided by ALICE Technologies, use machine learning to create optimized schedules and predict potential delays. These tools help reduce project durations and costs, improving overall project efficiency and success rates.

4. Safety Enhancement

AI improves safety by predicting hazards, monitoring compliance, and facilitating proactive interventions. Systems like Smartvid.io's Vinnie have reduced safety incidents by 30%, illustrating the potential for AI to create safer construction environments.

5. Quality Control

AI enhances quality control through real-time monitoring, automated inspections, and data-driven decision-making. Platforms like Buildots use computer vision to identify quality issues early, reducing rework and improving project quality.

6. Resource Optimization

AI optimizes resource allocation by predicting needs and reducing inefficiencies. Solutions like Versatile's CraneView have increased crane productivity by 20%, showcasing how AI can enhance the utilization of critical resources.

7. Scheduling

AI-driven scheduling tools analyze various project parameters to create efficient timelines and avoid delays. This ensures that projects are completed on time, reducing the risk of cost overruns and client dissatisfaction.

8. Site Monitoring

AI uses IoT devices and drones to provide real-time site monitoring, identifying issues before they escalate. This continuous oversight helps maintain project quality and safety, as exemplified by Skydio's autonomous drones.

9. Productivity Improvement

AI enhances productivity by automating repetitive tasks and optimizing workflows. Doxel's use of robotics and AI for progress tracking has increased productivity by 38%, demonstrating the significant impact of automation.

10. Profit Maximization

AI helps maximize profit by optimizing project management, resource allocation, cost control, and operational efficiency. AI-driven platforms like Oracle's Primavera Unifier provide real-time financial insights, reducing administrative costs and improving budget control.

Outlook for the Future

Integration of Advanced AI Technologies
The future of AI in construction will see the integration of more advanced technologies, such as deep learning, augmented reality (AR), and blockchain. Deep learning models will provide even more accurate predictions and insights, AR will enable enhanced visualization and planning, and blockchain will ensure transparency and security in procurement and contracts.

Widespread Adoption and Scalability
As AI technologies become more affordable and user-friendly, their adoption will become widespread, even among small and medium-sized construction firms. Scalable AI solutions will cater to projects of all sizes, democratizing access to advanced project management and optimization tools.

Enhanced Collaboration and Connectivity
AI will facilitate greater collaboration across the construction value chain by integrating various stakeholders through connected platforms. Real-time data sharing and collaboration tools will enable seamless communication and coordination, reducing delays and improving project outcomes.

Sustainability and Environmental Impact
AI will play a crucial role in promoting sustainability in construction. By optimizing resource usage, reducing waste, and enabling predictive maintenance, AI can help construction companies minimize their environmental footprint. AI-driven design tools will also allow for the creation of more energy-efficient and sustainable buildings.

Continuous Learning and Improvement
AI systems will continuously learn and improve from new data, leading to better performance over time. As more construction data

is collected and analyzed, AI algorithms will become increasingly accurate and reliable, further enhancing their value to the industry.

Human-AI Collaboration
The future will see a greater emphasis on human-AI collaboration, where AI systems augment human capabilities rather than replace them. Construction professionals will leverage AI to make more informed decisions, enhance their productivity, and focus on higher-value tasks.

Regulatory and Ethical Considerations
As AI becomes more prevalent in construction, there will be a need for clear regulatory frameworks and ethical guidelines to ensure its responsible use. Policymakers and industry leaders will need to collaborate to address issues such as data privacy, security, and the impact of AI on employment.

Conclusion

The transformative impact of AI on the construction industry is undeniable. From enhancing procurement efficiency and cost estimating to improving safety, quality control, and profit maximization, AI-driven technologies are reshaping how construction projects are planned, executed, and managed. Real-world examples and case studies highlight the tangible benefits of AI, including reduced costs, improved safety, enhanced quality, and increased productivity.

Looking forward, the integration of advanced AI technologies, widespread adoption, enhanced collaboration, sustainability initiatives, continuous learning, and human-AI collaboration will further revolutionize the construction industry. As AI continues to evolve, its potential to drive innovation, efficiency, and profitability in construction will only grow, ensuring that the industry is well-equipped to meet the challenges and opportunities of the future.

List of Companies Revolutionizing the Construction Industry with AI

This is a list of all the companies mentioned throughout the chapters, highlighting their contributions to revolutionizing various aspects of the construction industry with AI technologies. Each entry includes a brief introduction and the company's website address for further reference.

1. Katerra
Introduction: Katerra is a technology-driven offsite construction company that leverages AI to optimize procurement and supply chain management, ensuring cost-effective and timely delivery of materials.
Website: www.katerra.com

2. ALICE Technologies
Introduction: ALICE Technologies provides an AI-driven construction planning and scheduling platform that uses machine learning to generate optimized construction schedules and predict potential delays.
Website: www.alicetechnologies.com

3. ProEst
Introduction: ProEst is an AI-powered cost estimation platform that analyzes historical cost data and market trends to provide accurate budget forecasts and improve financial planning.
Website: www.proest.com

4. Smartvid.io
Introduction: Smartvid.io offers an AI-based safety platform named Vinnie, which uses machine learning to analyze site data, predict hazards, and enhance safety compliance.
Website: www.smartvid.io

5. Buildots
Introduction: Buildots utilizes computer vision and AI to monitor construction quality in real-time, identifying deviations from design specifications and ensuring project quality.
Website: www.buildots.com

6. Versatile
Introduction: Versatile's CraneView platform uses AI to optimize crane operations on construction sites, improving resource utilization and reducing operational costs.
Website: www.versatile.ai

7. Skydio
Introduction: Skydio manufactures autonomous drones equipped with AI for automated inspections of construction sites, enhancing accuracy and efficiency in defect detection.
Website: www.skydio.com

8. Oracle (Primavera Unifier)
Introduction: Oracle's Primavera Unifier is an AI-driven project management and financial control platform that automates financial processes and provides real-time insights into project finances.
Website: www.oracle.com

9. Doxel
Introduction: Doxel uses AI and robotics for progress tracking and quality control on construction sites, automating these processes to improve productivity and reduce project timelines.
Website: www.doxel.ai

10. Project Frog (KitConnect)
Introduction: Project Frog's KitConnect platform leverages AI to optimize supply chain management, ensuring timely and cost-effective material procurement for construction projects.
Website: www.projectfrog.com

11. Autodesk (BIM 360)
Introduction: Autodesk's BIM 360 platform utilizes AI to analyze construction data, providing insights into quality trends,

performance metrics, and recommendations for quality improvements.
Website: www.autodesk.com

12. nPlan
Introduction: nPlan's predictive analytics platform uses AI to analyze historical project data and predict potential quality issues, helping companies proactively manage quality and mitigate risks.
Website: www.nplan.io

13. Autodesk
Introduction: Autodesk is a leader in design software, providing tools for generative design and BIM (Building Information Modeling). Their AI-driven solutions help optimize office building layouts and improve energy efficiency.
Website: [autodesk.com](https://www.autodesk.com)

The Living
Introduction: A subsidiary of Autodesk, The Living uses generative design to create innovative and efficient architectural solutions, as seen in the design of Autodesk's Toronto office.
Website: [theliving.newyork](https://www.theliving.newyork)

Sidewalk Labs
Introduction: An Alphabet subsidiary, Sidewalk Labs is focused on developing smart cities with AI-driven design optimization to enhance sustainability and efficiency.
Website: [sidewalklabs.com](https://www.sidewalklabs.com)

Arup
Introduction: A global engineering firm, Arup employs AI to optimize structural designs, reducing material usage and enhancing resilience in projects like the Singapore Sports Hub.
Website: [arup.com](https://www.arup.com)

MX3D
Introduction: MX3D uses AI-driven generative design and robotic 3D printing to create innovative structures like the MX3D Bridge in Amsterdam, optimizing material usage and structural performance.

Website: [mx3d.com](https://www.mx3d.com)

Google (TensorFlow)
Introduction: Google's TensorFlow is a powerful machine learning platform used in construction for analyzing historical data and predicting optimal design strategies.
Website: [tensorflow.org](https://www.tensorflow.org)

Microsoft (Azure Machine Learning)
Introduction: Microsoft's Azure Machine Learning platform helps construction companies predict optimal design strategies and identify potential issues through data analysis.
Website: azure.microsoft.com

ANSYS Fluent
Introduction: ANSYS Fluent provides CFD (Computational Fluid Dynamics) tools to simulate airflow and thermal performance, optimizing building designs for natural ventilation and energy efficiency.
Website: [ansys.com](https://www.ansys.com)

SimScale
Introduction: SimScale offers cloud-based CFD tools for optimizing building designs, improving energy efficiency and indoor comfort through AI-driven simulations.
Website: [simscale.com](https://www.simscale.com)

Bentley Systems (GenerativeComponents)
Introduction: Bentley Systems provides GenerativeComponents, an AI-driven generative design tool that explores numerous design possibilities for optimal solutions.
Website: [bentley.com](https://www.bentley.com)

Tekla
Introduction: Tekla's software integrates AI algorithms for structural optimization, enhancing the efficiency and durability of building designs.
Website: [tekla.com](https://www.tekla.com)

SAP2000

Introduction: SAP2000 offers structural optimization algorithms that reduce material usage while maintaining structural integrity, used in various engineering projects.
Website:[csiamerica.com](https://www.csiamerica.com/products/sap2000)

EnergyPlus

Introduction: EnergyPlus provides energy modeling and simulation tools, enabling AI-driven optimization for energy-efficient building designs.
Website: [energyplus.net](https://www.energyplus.net)

OpenStudio

Introduction: OpenStudio offers energy modeling tools that integrate AI simulations to identify the most energy-efficient building configurations.
Website: [openstudio.net](https://www.openstudio.net)

This list showcases the diversity and innovation within the construction industry, highlighting how AI is being utilized by various companies to drive efficiency, safety, quality, and profitability. For more information on each company and their AI solutions, please visit their respective websites.

www.ingramcontent.com/pod-product-compliance
Lightning Source LLC
Chambersburg PA
CBHW050014230526
45470CB00003B/965